North Carolina

Rich Smith

Visit us at
www.abdopublishing.com

Printed in the United States.

Editor: John Hamilton
Graphic Design: Sue Hamilton
Cover Illustration: Neil Klinepier
Cover Photo: iStock Photo
Interior Photo Credits: 20th Century Fox, Alamy, AP Images, Carolina Hurricanes, Carolina Panthers, Charlotte Bobcats, Corbis, Getty, Granger Collection, iStock Photo, Jupiterimages, Library of Congress, Mile High Maps, Mountain High Maps, North Carolina Research Institute, Sony Pictures, One Mile Up, U.S. Coast Guard, and White House Historical Association.
Statistics: State population statistics taken from 2008 U.S. Census Bureau estimates. City and town population statistics taken from July 1, 2007, U.S. Census Bureau estimates. Land and water area statistics taken from 2000 Census, U.S. Census Bureau.

Manufactured with paper containing at least 10% post-consumer waste

Library of Congress Cataloging-in-Publication Data

Smith, Rich, 1954-
  North Carolina / Rich Smith.
      p. cm. -- (The United States)
  Includes index.
  ISBN 978-1-60453-668-3
  1. North Carolina--Juvenile literature. I. Title.

F254.3.S63 2010
975.6--dc22
                                    2008052319

Table of Contents

The Tar Heel State

 North Carolina is an Atlantic Ocean coastal state in the southeastern region of the United States. Its vast pine forests once provided tar and pitch for sealing the wood on ships. The Tar Heel State may refer to this sticky tar and the people whose feet walked through it.

 For years, the state was mostly farm country. Today, North Carolina is better known as a place for science and technology. That change began even before the Wright Brothers flew the first powered airplane on a North Carolina beach more than 100 years ago.

 North Carolina is beautiful. It has long beaches and towering mountains. It has endless forests and grassy marshes. There are gorgeous skies and clear waters. So many people want to live in North Carolina, it has become one of the nation's fastest-growing states.

Built in 1869, the Cape Hatteras Lighthouse is the tallest lighthouse in America. It is 208 feet (63 m) tall, has 268 steps, and its light can be seen for more than 20 miles (32 km).

Quick Facts

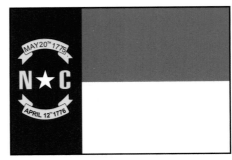

Name: North Carolina was named in honor of King Charles I of England.

State Capital: Raleigh, population 375,806

Date of Statehood: November 21, 1789 (12th state)

Population: 9,222,414 (10th-most populous state)

Area (Total Land and Water): 53,819 square miles (139,391 sq km), the 28th-largest state

Largest City: Charlotte, population 671,588

Nicknames: The Tar Heel State or The Old North State

Motto: *Esse quam videri* (To be rather than to seem)

State Bird: Cardinal

Mount Mitchell

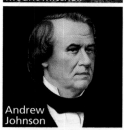

Andrew Johnson

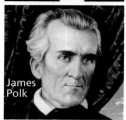

James Polk

State Flower: Dogwood

State Rock: Granite

State Tree: Longleaf Pine

State Song: "The Old North State"

Highest Point: 6,684 feet (2,037 m), Mount Mitchell

Lowest Point: 0 feet (0 m), Atlantic Ocean

Average July Temperature: 77°F (25°C)

Record High Temperature: 110°F (43°C) in Fayetteville, August 21, 1983,

Average January Temperature: 40°F (4°C)

Record Low Temperature: -34°F (-37°C) on Mount Mitchell, January 21, 1985

Average Annual Precipitation: 50 inches (127 cm)

Number of U.S. Senators: 2

Number of U.S. Representatives: 13

U.S. Presidents Born in North Carolina: Andrew Johnson, James Polk

U.S. Postal Service Abbreviation: NC

Geography

North Carolina is located along the East Coast of the southern United States. Its neighbor to the north is Virginia. To the west is Tennessee. Georgia and South Carolina are to the south. The Atlantic Ocean lies to the east.

North Carolina covers 53,819 square miles (139,391 sq km). It is the 28th-largest state.

The state has three natural regions. The one nearest the Atlantic Ocean is a low coastal plain. It extends inland to nearly the middle of the state. Much of the plain closest to the shoreline is covered by marshes. These marshes are shielded from ocean waves by a string of sand barrier islands called the Outer Banks.

North Carolina's total land and water area is 53,819 square miles (139,391 sq km). It is the 28th-largest state. The state capital is Raleigh.

West of the coastal plain is the Piedmont region. It covers one-third of the state and is mostly a plateau. The boundary between the Piedmont and the coastal plain is known as the fall line. It is named that because the edge of the Piedmont drops almost straight down a few hundred feet where it meets the coastal plain. Geologists believe the edge of the Piedmont in ancient times was North Carolina's shoreline.

Farthest west is the Appalachian Mountain region. Mountain ranges within the Appalachians are called subranges. These include the Blue Ridge, Great Smoky, Great Balsam, Black, and Pisgah Mountains. The state's highest point is in this region. It is Mount Mitchell, at 6,684 feet (2,037 m).

The most important rivers are the Roanoke, Tar, Neuse, Cape Fear, Yadkin, Catawba, and French Broad. The largest natural lakes are Mattamuskeet, Phelps, and Waccamaw.

North Carolina's Blue Ridge Parkway shows the reason for its name with the beautiful Blue Ridge Mountains stretching across the area. The Blue Ridge Mountains are a subrange within the Appalachian Mountains.

Climate and Weather

North Carolina's coastal plain is warmed in the winter and cooled in the summer by air blowing from the Atlantic Ocean.

A sudden snowstorm strikes a man in Boone, North Carolina.

The Piedmont region is too far inland to be affected by the Atlantic Ocean. Its winters are colder, and summers warmer, than the coastal plain.

The high altitude of the Appalachian Mountains makes the far west of the state very cold in winter and cool in the summer.

The average temperature for the entire state in January is about 40°F (4°C). In July it is about 77°F (25°C).

Rain falls throughout the year, but it is driest in the autumn. Precipitation statewide averages 50 inches (127 cm) annually. Rain along the east slopes of the big mountains measures more than 90 inches (229 cm) each year. The mountains receive up to 20 inches (51 cm) of snow in a typical winter. Hurricanes hit the state about once every 10 years. About 20 tornados strike the state each year.

Heavy rains cause a creek to flood, endangering a log home in Bat Cave, North Carolina.

Plants and Animals

Each of North Carolina's three regions is home to different kinds of plants and animals. The marshes of the coastal plain contain cordgrass. Many of the sandy dunes along the beaches are covered in sea oats. The coastal region also has many swamps that give rise to graceful cypress trees.

Sea oats grow on North Carolina's sandy dunes.

The low end of the Piedmont region has several kinds of pine trees. In the higher end grow oak and hickory trees. In between the two ends are many poplar trees.

Toward the bottom of the Appalachian region are sugar maple, yellow birch, beech, and many other beautiful trees. Up high are spruce and fir trees.

A cardinal, North Carolina's state bird, sits in a pine tree.

The Carolina wren sings a loud song that sounds like "tea-kettle, tea-kettle, tea-kettle."

The rivers and lakes of North Carolina contain fish such as trout, bass, perch, pickerel, and catfish. In the waters of the Atlantic are flounder and bluefish.

Birds of North Carolina include mourning dove, wild turkey, bobwhite quail, and many more. The cardinal is the state's official bird.

Alligators live in the swamps and lakes of the coastal plain. The Great Smoky Mountains are home to black bears. One of the most familiar forest animals in North Carolina is the white-tailed deer. Wild boars, beavers, and bobcats also live in the state.

White-tailed deer are found in North Carolina's forests.

Bear

Oystercatcher with Oyster

Wild Boar

History

More than 15 major Native American tribes lived in North Carolina by the time explorer Giovanni da Verrazzano of Italy set foot there in 1524. Beginning in 1584, Sir Walter Raleigh of England tried to set up colonies two different

A 1585 sketch of a Native American Algonquian village near today's Gibbs Creek, North Carolina. Huts and longhouses sit inside a protective fence.

times in North Carolina. Both attempts failed. The worst failure was the second try. About 120 settlers vanished from Roanoke Island in the Outer Banks. Their disappearance remains a mystery.

The first successful European settlements of North Carolina were those started by colonists who came from neighboring Virginia in the 1650s. At first, local Native Americans were tolerant of the settlers. But by 1710, they wanted no more whites coming onto Indian land. The Indians went to war against the settlers. The fighting lasted four years and ended in defeat for the Indians. More settlers arrived. In 1729, the king of England changed some laws so that it would be easier for people to buy land in North Carolina. That triggered an even bigger flood of settlers.

An early settlement at Roanoke Island.

Many early European settlers paid their way to North Carolina by agreeing to become indentured servants. Others who came to North Carolina were African slaves. They were forced to do backbreaking work in the colony's tobacco and cotton fields.

This tolerance of slavery was strange, because North Carolina in 1776 was the first American colony to formally demand freedom from Great Britain. Most of the battles between the colonists and Britain in North Carolina during the Revolutionary War were minor. But they did play an important part in defeating the British. After the war, North Carolina became the 12th state when it approved the United States Constitution on November 21, 1789.

In 1861, North Carolina was on the side of the slave-owning southern states when the Civil War broke out.

However, North Carolina had far fewer slaves than most of the other rebel states. That is partly because many slave owners were convinced by Christian preachers to voluntarily free their slaves. But other slave owners held onto their slaves until they were forced by the armies of the victorious Union to let them go.

Union troops force Southern owners to free the slaves in 1864.

A lesson North Carolina learned from the Civil War was that it needed to stop being so heavily dependent on farming. In the 1880s, the state began industrializing. It started by building cotton mills. By the 1920s, those mills made more fabric than anyplace else in America.

Inside a Cherryville, North Carolina, cotton mill in 1908. Before child labor laws, mills often hired young people to do the work.

NORTH CAROLINA

The success of the cotton mills opened the door to more industrialization. And industrialization led to modernization. Today, North Carolina is a leader in scientific research and technology.

The Hearst Tower is home to many different businesses in Charlotte, North Carolina.

Did You Know?

- Mount Mitchell is the tallest peak in North Carolina. It is also the tallest peak in the United States east of the Mississippi River.

- The most feared pirate of the high seas was Blackbeard. He made his home for a time in North Carolina. Blackbeard was killed at Ocracoke Island on the Outer Banks in a battle with the British navy. Legend has it that Blackbeard's headless body swam around his ship several times before finally vanishing under the water.

- It is hard to find waters more dangerous than those east of North Carolina's Outer Banks. This area is called the Graveyard of the Atlantic. More than 2,000 ships since the 1500s sank there.

- The first controlled flight of a powered airplane took place in North Carolina on December 17, 1903. The plane was built by Wilbur and Orville Wright. They flew it off Big Kill Devil Hill, near the town of Kitty Hawk, North Carolina. Orville piloted the first flight, which lasted only 12 seconds and covered a distance of 120 feet (37 m).

People

Daniel Boone (1734-1820) helped open the United States frontier. His wilderness adventures made him one of the first and most famous American folk heroes. Boone was born in Pennsylvania, but grew up near the North Carolina town of Mocksville.

Dolley Madison (1768-1849) was married to James Madison, the fourth president of the United States. Dolley Madison is best remembered for bravely rescuing treasures from the White House just before the British army burned it during the War of 1812. She was born in Guilford County.

Levi Coffin (1798-1877) was a teacher who helped slaves escape to freedom in the years before the Civil War. The number of slaves he aided was thought to be around 3,000. After the Civil War, Coffin raised money to help feed, clothe, and shelter former slaves who had not yet learned how to live as free men and women. Coffin was born in Greensboro, North Carolina.

William Sydney Porter (1862-1910) was a favorite American writer of short stories. His pen name was O. Henry. He wrote the first handful of his nearly 400 tales while in prison. Readers enjoyed O. Henry stories because they usually ended with a surprise twist. Porter was born in Greensboro, North Carolina.

Richard Gatling invented the rapid-fire Gatling gun in 1861.

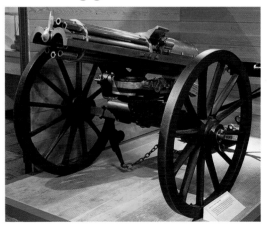

Richard J. Gatling (1818-1903) invented the first successful machine gun. His Gatling gun helped the Union Army defeat the South during the Civil War. A later version of his weapon was used in the famous charge up Cuba's San Juan Hill during the Spanish-American War. Gatling invented many other things besides the machine gun. Among them was one of the first motorized farm tractors. Gatling was born in Hertford County.

Edward R. Murrow

(1908-1965) was a legend in the field of American broadcast journalism. He reported by radio from London for CBS News during the worst of the nightly

Nazi bombing raids at the beginning of World War II. He moved from radio to television after the war. He reported on many of the most important events of the day. Murrow was born near Greensboro.

Cities

The largest city in North Carolina is **Charlotte**. Its population is about 671,588. Only four other cities along the entire East Coast of America are more populated. The city is a major center of finance. Several of the nation's biggest banks are headquartered in Charlotte. The city was founded in 1768. It is named for a German princess who married England's King George III. Charlotte's nickname is The Queen City.

The capital of North Carolina is **Raleigh**. It is also the state's second-largest city. Raleigh's population is about 375,806. The city was founded in 1792. It is named after Sir Walter Raleigh of England. He was the nobleman who sponsored the first attempts at colonizing North Carolina in the late 1500s. The city today is a national leader in science and technology research.

Greensboro is located in the north-central part of the state. It is North Carolina's third-largest city, with a population of 247,183. Greensboro historically was a home for companies that made textiles and furniture. The city in recent years attracted a number of high-technology firms and transportation companies. Greensboro is named for Revolutionary War hero General Nathanael Greene.

The city of **Winston-Salem** has a population of 215,348. That makes it North Carolina's fourth-largest city. Until 1913, it was two separate cities. Salem was founded in 1766. Neighboring Winston was founded in 1849. Winston-Salem is located in the northwest-central part of the state. Tobacco was a major industry in the city for many years. Other important industries today include food processing, finance, and medicine.

Transportation

North Carolina has one of the nation's biggest and best road systems. There are nearly 100,000 miles (160,934 km) of roads connecting North Carolina's cities. The state also has a very well developed system of mass transit.

More than 23 million people each year use ferries to reach the islands of the Outer Banks. The state has one of the largest ferry systems in the nation.

The airports of North Carolina are often busy. About 47 million passengers each year use the state's 9 major airports and nearly 300 smaller airports.

Each year, about 580,000 people travel by railroad in North Carolina. Freight trains annually haul well over 100 million tons (91 million metric tons) of cargo.

Ocracoke Ferry transports people and vehicles back and forth from Hatteras to Ocracoke.

North Carolina has one the country's biggest and best road systems. Vast numbers of people travel across the state's roadways to view the beauty of North Carolina.

Natural Resources

Sweet
Potatoes

North Carolina is one of the most important farm states in the nation. More than one-third of the sweet potatoes grown in America come from North Carolina. The same is true of tobacco. The state is also a leading producer of cucumbers, peppers, peanuts, cabbage, eggplant, blueberries, and beans. The state also ranks high for raising hogs and poultry.

Many useful minerals are mined in North Carolina. These include olivine lithium, phosphate rock, kaolin, and industrial gravel. The state leads the nation in the mining of feldspar, mica, pyrophyllite, and common clay.

The waters of North Carolina yield big catches of trout, catfish, flounder, shrimp, crabs, and clams.

Forests cover nearly two-thirds of North Carolina. That helps explain why the state is among the nation's top producers of lumber.

With its vast forests, North Carolina is among the country's top producers of lumber.

Industry

North Carolina once was known for textiles, paper, furniture, and chemicals. Today, there are fewer of these industries because of competition from outside the United States. But that has not stopped the state from enjoying a healthy economy. Many new types of industries have sprung up or moved into North Carolina to take the place of those that have closed or gone away. Among the most recent additions are finance, transportation, scientific exploration, high-technology, medicine, and education.

In 2006, a closed textile mill is torn down in Kannapolis, North Carolina. In its place today is the North Carolina Research Campus, a modern institute for scientific study.

A surprise to some is that quite a few Hollywood movies and television programs are made in North Carolina. Film studios are located in seven North Carolina cities. Some popular movies produced in the state include *Talladega Nights*, *Shallow Hal*, *28 Days*, *Evil Dead 2*, *The Crow*, *Cape Fear*, and *Dirty Dancing*.

Many film studios are located in North Carolina. Several popular movies have been shot in the state, including *Talladega Nights* and *Shallow Hal.*

Sports

Fans of the National Football League enjoy the games played by the Carolina Panthers. The Panthers play their home games in Charlotte.

The National Basketball Association is represented by the Charlotte Bobcats. This team was formed in 2004 to replace the Charlotte Hornets.

The National Hockey League's Carolina Hurricanes play out of Raleigh. In 2006, the Hurricanes won the Stanley Cup.

North Carolina also is home to teams playing professional soccer and indoor football.

Rockingham Speedway is a racetrack in the city of Rockingham. Its nickname is "The Rock."

There are a number of minor-league baseball teams. Professional golf tournaments come to the state several times each year. Beloved by many North Carolinians are off-road motorcycling and stock-car racing events. Basketball is the most-watched college sport.

North Carolina's beautiful wilderness parks allow residents to enjoy hiking, camping, and many other outdoor activities.

Entertainment

The North Carolina Symphony is the state's full-time, professional orchestra. It gives 175 concerts per year. More than 40 of those are performed free to audiences made up almost entirely of schoolchildren. The symphony appears most of the time at Raleigh's beautiful Meymandi Concert Hall.

The North Carolina Museum of Art is located in Raleigh. It displays fine collections of American, European, African, and Pacific Island art.

There are more than 175 museums and historical sites located in North Carolina. The state's public library system has about 75 locations and offers more than 14 million volumes to the public.

A popular North Carolina historic site is the Wright Brothers National Memorial at Kill Devil Hills. A bronze and steel statue remembers the world's first powered flight. Orville Wright flew the aircraft for 12 seconds on December 17, 1903. The sculpture, created by Stephen Smith, was placed in 2003 to honor 100 years of flight.

Timeline

1524—Italian explorer Giovanni da Verrazzano lands in North Carolina.

1584—Sir Walter Raleigh given permission by Queen Elizabeth I of England to start colonies in North Carolina.

1650s—Virginians start first successful settlements in North Carolina.

1714—Native American tribes lose a four-year war against white settlers.

1776—North Carolina is first of the 13 American colonies to demand freedom from British rule.

1789—North Carolina becomes the 12th state in the Union.

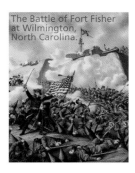

The Battle of Fort Fisher at Wilmington, North Carolina.

1861—Civil War starts. North Carolina joins the rebel Confederate States of America.

1865—North Carolina brought back into the Union at end of Civil War.

1903—First powered airplane flight at Kitty Hawk, North Carolina.

1970s—Modernization of North Carolina's economy begins with shift toward technology and science research.

2006—The Carolina Hurricanes win the National Hockey League's Stanley Cup.

Glossary

Barrier Islands—Long and narrow landforms just offshore from a mainland. Typically made up of sand, silt, or pebbles.

Civil War—The war fought between America's Northern and Southern states from 1861-1865. The Southern states were for slavery. They wanted to start their own country. Northern states fought against slavery and a division of the country.

Colony—A place settled by people from someplace else. Usually, the settlers remain under the control of the government of the place from which they came.

Indentured Servant—A person forced to work for someone to whom he or she owes money. The wages that would ordinarily be paid to the worker are instead kept by the employer as payment of the worker's debt. The worker is free to leave his or her employer once the debt is paid.

Industrialize—To change a society from one in which work is done mainly by hand to one in which work is done mainly by machines.

Outer Banks—A long string of barrier islands that extend for about 200 miles (322 km) along the northern coast of North Carolina. These sand-dune islands help to protect North Carolina's eastern coastline from the rough seas of the Atlantic Ocean. With its warm climate and long beaches, the Outer Banks area is also a popular place for tourists to visit.

Piedmont—An Italian word that means "at the foot of the hills."

Plateau—A large area of land that is mainly flat but much higher than the land that neighbors it.

Revolutionary War—The war fought between the American colonies and Great Britain from 1775-1783. It is also known as the American Revolution or the War of Independence.

Index

WITHDRAWN

**Indianapolis
Marion County
Public Library**

Renew by Phone
269-5222

Renew on the Web
www.imcpl.org

For General Library Information
please call 269-1700